THE STORY OF THE
SEATTLE
MARINERS

SEC.
14
ROW
8
SEAT
10

Used this
Ticket for
FOURTH GAME

GRANDSTAND SEAT $**6.00**
Est. Price $5.00 + Tax $1.00 = TOTAL

Right hereby reserved to refund sold price
and revoke license granted by this ticket.

GAME
4

DAY GAME
THE BALLPARK
★
American League
vs.
National League

Read Important
Notices on
Reverse Side
★
Do Not Detach
This Coupon From
Rain Check

GAME
4

RAIN CHECK

DAY GAME
GRANDSTAND SEAT
Est. Price $5.00 $**6.00**
Fed. Tax $1.00
TOTAL

Right hereby reserved to refund sold price and revoke
license granted by this ticket.

READ IMPORTANT NOTICES
ON REVERSE SIDE

GAME
4

SEC.
14
ROW
8
SEAT
10

Published by Creative Education
P.O. Box 227, Mankato, Minnesota 56002
Creative Education is an imprint of The Creative Company

Design and production by Blue Design
Printed in the United States of America

Photographs by Getty Images (KIMBERLY BARTH/AFP, Bernstein Associates, ANDREW CUTRARO/AFP, Jonathan Daniel/Stringer, Tomasso Derosa, Stephen Dunn, Stephen Dunn/Allsport, Charles Franklin/MLB Photos, Otto Greule Jr, Otto Greule Jr/Allsport, Jed Jacobsohn, Robert Leiter/MLB Photos, DAN LEVINE/AFP, DANIEL LIPPITT/AFP, Lonnie Major/Allsport, Brad Mangin/MLB Photos, Jim McIsaac, National Baseball Hall of Fame Library/MLB Photos, Richard T. Nowitz/National Geographic, Doug Pensinger, Rich Pilling/MLB Photos, John Reid III/MLB Photos, Rick Stewart, Rick Stewart/Allsport, YOSHIKAZU TSUNO/AFP, John Williamson/MLB Photos), National Baseball Hall of Fame Library, Cooperstown, N.Y.

Library of Congress Cataloging-in-Publication Data

Peterson, Sheryl.
The story of the Seattle Mariners / by Sheryl Peterson.
p. cm. — (Baseball: the great American game)
Includes index.
ISBN-13: 978-1-58341-500-9
1. Seattle Mariners (Baseball team)—History—Juvenile literature. I. Title. II. Series.

GV875.S42P48 2007
796.357'6409797772—dc22   2006027459

First Edition
9 8 7 6 5 4 3 2 1

Cover: Third baseman Edgar Martinez
Page 1: Outfielder Ichiro Suzuki
Page 3: Third baseman Adrian Beltre

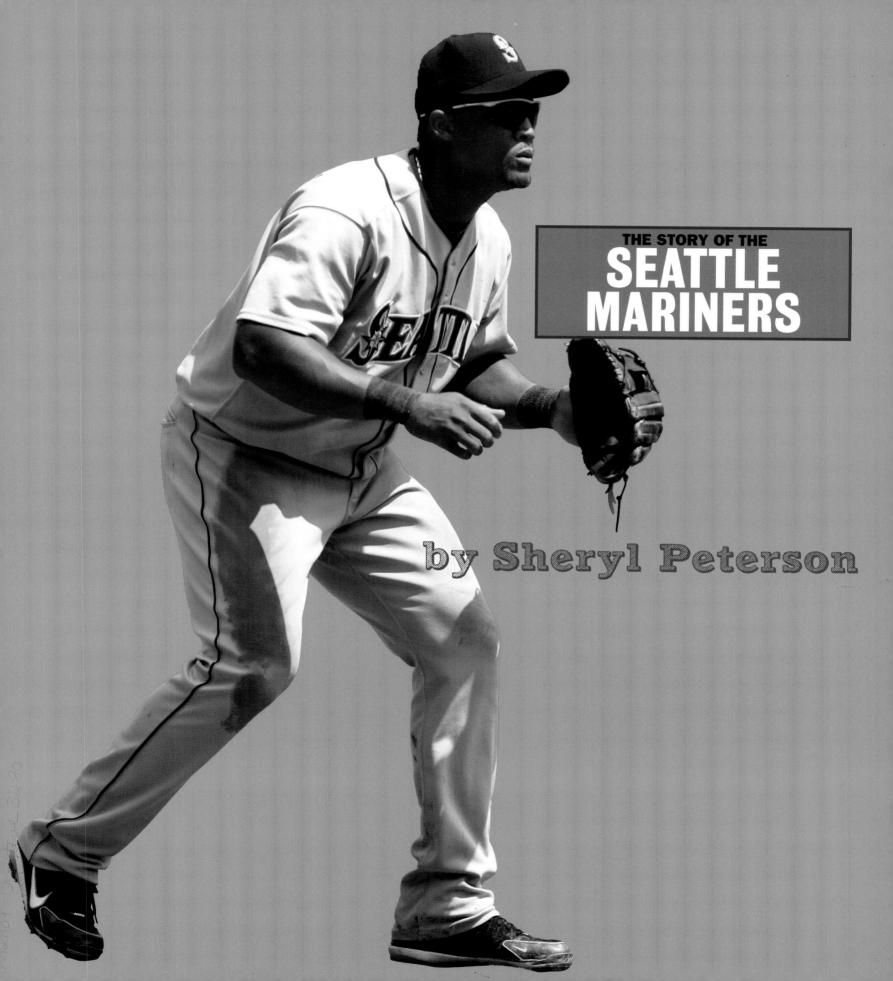

THE STORY OF THE
SEATTLE MARINERS

by Sheryl Peterson

THE STORY OF THE
Seattle Mariners

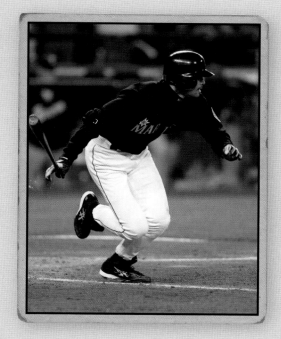

Hit number 258 for Seattle Mariners right fielder Ichiro Suzuki was just a little ground ball straight up the middle like so many others, but with one huge difference: this hit made baseball history. Sparkling fireworks exploded in the Seattle sky, creating a haze over Safeco Field, and Ichiro's teammates mobbed him at first base. Across the Pacific Ocean, in Ichiro's native Japan, fans cheered wildly in front of wide-screen monitors in downtown Tokyo. Hit number 258 on October 1, 2004, had just broken the major-league record for the most hits in a season, a mark that had been held by baseball great George Sisler for 84 years. With adoring Seattle spectators chanting "I-chi-ro!, I-chi-ro!" the new hero ran over to the seats along the first-base line, bowed respectfully in Japanese tradition, and shook hands with Sisler's daughter. Flashbulbs popped to capture the moment— just the latest in a long line of baseball highlights in the Pacific Northwest.

HOME-TEAM HARBOR

Between white-capped mountains and the silvery blue water of Puget Sound lies the city of Seattle, Washington. Because of the lush evergreen trees native to the area, Seattle's official nickname is "The Emerald City." Seattle, the largest city in the Pacific Northwest region of the United States, maintains a busy shipping, tour boat, and cruise ship harbor. The Space Needle, a futuristic structure built for the 1962 World's Fair, continues to be the city's most famous tourist attraction.

Seattle boasts a picturesque setting, but its first experience with major league baseball wasn't nearly as pretty. In 1969, the Seattle Pilots, a Northwest baseball experiment, played at a renovated minor-league park called Sick's Stadium. The team finished its inaugural season in last place in the American League (AL) Western Division with a record of 64–98 and then, due to money problems, was moved to Milwaukee and renamed the Brewers.

After that, rainy Seattle endured a pro baseball drought for seven years until another AL franchise was awarded to the city in 1976. The new club weighed anchor at the Kingdome, the first domed ballpark in the league. Fans

Seattle was settled in 1851 and is today known for its many coffee companies and jet manufacturing industry.

ONE-YEAR WONDERS

Seattle's first big-league baseball team was the Pilots, named in commemoration of the area's maritime and aviation history. The Pilots joined the AL in 1969, but by the next season, they had been moved and reborn as the Milwaukee Brewers. The club was an oddity as the only major-league team in decades to relocate after just a single season. It had happened once before in the 20th century—ironically, to the original Milwaukee Brewers, who became the St. Louis Browns after the 1901 season. The Pilots were also the first major-league team to declare bankruptcy, mostly due to low fan attendance at games. The club's home opener was attended by Washington governor Dan Evans, AL president Joe Cronin, and even famous cowboy actor Gene Autry. Basking in the limelight, the Pilots beat the Chicago White Sox 7–0. But ticket prices were among the highest in baseball, the home-field Sick's Stadium was in bad condition, and injuries plagued the team as it lost 22 of 28 games in August. Interest in the Pilots has grown in recent years, due in part to the 1970 book *Ball Four* by pitcher Jim Bouton that offers an insider's look at the team and has become something of a classic.

were polled by a local newspaper for a team name and overwhelmingly selected "Mariners" (sometimes shortened to "M's" by the media), since many locals loved boating on their scenic ocean bay. Uniforms were soon unveiled that featured the seaside colors of emerald green, navy blue, and silver.

The Mariners made a speedy outfielder named Ruppert Jones their first pick in the 1976 major-league expansion draft. Other key players signed included veteran outfielder Leroy Stanton, who would crack 27 home runs and drive in 90 runs in 1977, and swift, base-stealing second baseman Julio Cruz. The new club played its first game on April 6, 1977, in front of a sold-out crowd at the Kingdome. On the mound was Diego Segui, a Cuban right-hander who had played for the Seattle Pilots. Unfortunately, the game ended in a 7–0 whitewash at the hands of the California Angels.

Diehard Seattle fans got fired up each time Jones came to the plate wielding his booming bat that first season. When "Take Me Out to the Ballgame" was played in the Kingdome, baseball fans "Rupe, Rupe, Ruped!" for the Mariners, changing the lyrics to express their adulation for Jones, who earned a spot on the 1977 AL All-Star team. Despite Jones's efforts and those of Stanton and Cruz, Seattle's opening season was one of many defeats, and the team finished the year 64–98, second-to-last in the AL West.

In 1978, first baseman Bruce Bochte joined the team and became an instant star, hitting well above .300. And the Mariners were lucky for it. "In the

PITCHER · RANDY JOHNSON

With his penetrating scowl, enormous wingspan, and tendency to unleash a wild pitch now and then, Johnson was arguably the most intimidating man ever to set foot on a pitcher's mound. At 6-foot-10, he was also the tallest pitcher ever to play in the major leagues. Johnson's nearly 100-mile-per-hour heater, combined with a brutal slider, made "The Big Unit" a devastating power pitcher for the better part of two decades. In 1995, one of the best years of his Mariners career, the rangy southpaw hurled a complete-game three-hitter that clinched Seattle's first-ever division title and first postseason appearance.

STATS

Mariners seasons: 1989–98

Height: 6-10

Weight: 225

- **10-time All-Star**
- **5-time Cy Young Award winner**
- **3.22 career ERA**
- **4-time AL leader in strikeouts**

RANDY JOHNSON
PITCHER

SEATTLE
MARINERS

beginning, I was the only one hitting the ball," Bochte later recalled. "It got to the point that I felt if I didn't get two hits and drive in two runs, we wouldn't win the game." The pressure seemed to send Bochte into a slump, and the Mariners ended the season in last place.

Things improved in 1979 when slick-hitting left fielder Willie Horton came aboard and clubbed 29 home runs. Seattle hosted baseball's annual All-Star Game that year, and local hero Bochte drove in a run in the "Midseason Classic" and posted 100 runs batted in (RBI) during the regular season, helping the Mariners capture 11 more wins than they had in 1978.

The 1980 and 1981 seasons were disappointments, as even the fine ef-

WILLIE HORTON

WILLIE HORTON — Like many of the team's early players, Horton was in the twilight of his career when he arrived in Seattle. The stocky outfielder, who had played for three different teams in 1978, surprised many people with 29 homers and 106 RBI in 1979.

forts of lefty hurler Floyd Bannister, outfielders Jeff Burroughs and Dave Henderson, and the ever-productive Bochte could not keep the club from backsliding. California real estate tycoon George Argyros purchased the team in 1981 and quickly reduced salaries, making his players among the lowest-paid in the majors. As the Mariners ended the strike-shortened 1981 season with only 44 wins, cheers were few in Seattle.

In 1982, under new manager Rene Lachemann, the Mariners began to shore up their pitching staff. Perhaps the most prominent name in the rotation was Gaylord Perry, who had already spent 20 seasons in the big leagues and acquired the nickname "The Ancient Mariner" in Seattle. That season, the 42-year-old Perry celebrated his 300th career win. Perry, who would eventually enter the Baseball Hall of Fame, was a notorious spitballer (a pitcher who illegally spits on the ball before throwing it) and was once quoted as saying, "I reckon I tried everything on the old apple but salt and pepper and chocolate sauce topping." Bannister led the league in strikeouts in 1982 with his fiery fastball, and relief pitchers Bill Caudill and Ed Vande Berg helped boost the Mariners' record to 76–86.

The Mariners spent the mid-1980s trying to add young talent. In 1984, first baseman Alvin Davis swung a loaded bat, finishing the season with 27 home

The ball moved unpredictably after leaving Gaylord Perry's hand, resulting in an AL-high 13 wild pitches in 1982.

GAYLORD PERRY

CATCHER · DAN WILSON

As a young Cincinnati Reds fan growing up in Chicago, Wilson spent time in elementary school drawing catchers in his notebooks and worshipping Reds backstop Johnny Bench. His dream of making it to the big leagues came true when he joined the Mariners in 1994. After a slow 1995 season, Wilson's natural talents emerged when the feisty catcher earned more playing time, slammed 18 home runs, and made the 1996 All-Star team. But defense was really Wilson's specialty, as he threw out 43 percent of would-be base stealers and led the AL in putouts at catcher in 1996.

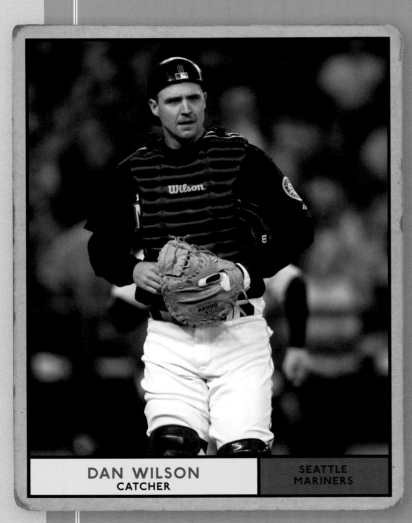

DAN WILSON
CATCHER

SEATTLE
MARINERS

STATS

Mariners seasons: 1994–2005

Height: 6-3

Weight: 200

- **88 career HR**

- **519 career RBI**

- **1996 All-Star**

- **.995 career fielding percentage**

runs and 116 RBI. Crafty southpaw pitcher Mark Langston, meanwhile, combined sneaky curveballs and steaming heaters that season to become the first rookie in 30 years to lead the AL in strikeouts, fanning 204 batters.

Injuries plagued the Mariners in 1985 and 1986, but loyal fans still saw highlights. On opening day of 1986, for example, clutch-hitting third baseman Jim Presley clouted a 10th-inning, game-winning grand slam (this after he tied the game with a two-run homer in the ninth). Despite such individual feats, the Mariners posted their 10th straight losing record in 1986, and fan attendance at the Kingdome waned. Seattle needed some heroes.

MARK LANGSTON

MARK LANGSTON – The hard-throwing lefty was one of baseball's elite pitchers in the late 1980s, leading the league in strikeouts in three of his six seasons (1984–89) in a Mariners uniform. Langston also set a club record with his 19 victories in 1987.

EDGAR MARTINEZ

EDGAR MARTINEZ – Martinez was slow to develop as a pro, spending much of his time in Seattle's minor-league system from 1982 to 1989. He played as a designated hitter for most of his career and excelled in the role, topping the 100 RBI mark in six seasons.

MARINERS SET SAIL

A new sense of optimism took hold in Seattle in 1987 as the Mariners produced a then-club-record 78 wins behind All-Stars Langston, Presley, and second baseman Harold Reynolds. Langston won 19 games with a 3.84 earned run average (ERA), while the speedy Reynolds stole a club-record 60 bases. Reynolds won the Gold Glove award the next year despite leading all AL second basemen in errors, since he also led the league in assists and double plays. The award made headlines as perennial honoree Frank White of the Kansas City Royals was livid at the selection, putting Reynolds in an uncomfortable position. "I was totally shocked to win the Gold Glove," Reynolds admitted. "But what was I supposed to do? Give it back?"

The Mariners really seemed ready to set sail after rookie third baseman Edgar Martinez joined the squad during the 1987 season. The slugging right-hander would bat over .300 in his first three full seasons in Seattle. When the soft-spoken Martinez stepped into the batter's box and cocked his bat back, Mariners fans would come alive with the boisterous chant, "Ed-Grrrrrr." As Minnesota Twins star Kirby Puckett once helpfully told a reporter who was writing about Martinez, "You can save a lot of room in your column by just saying three words: hit, hit, hit."

Still, Mariners owner George Argyros was becoming impatient. "We are no longer an expansion team," he said. "It's time we started winning." In 1988, strapping outfielder Jay Buhner, nicknamed "Bone" because of his shaved head, came to Seattle from the New York Yankees. Buhner later joked about the lack of attendance at home games, recalling, "The Kingdome was so empty you could hear the crickets chirping from the upper decks."

In 1989, the Mariners traded Langston and replaced him with a towering, young, left-handed pitcher named Randy Johnson. Also new to the roster that season was effervescent, 19-year-old center fielder Ken Griffey Jr., known to fans simply as "Junior." Griffey had it all: brilliant defensive skills, effortless speed, and prodigious hitting power. In 11 seasons with the Mariners, Griffey would become one of baseball's most popular stars of the 1990s and spark the team to increasing success. "I don't think anybody has ever been that good at that age," said Mariners batting coach Gene Clines.

In a dominant performance, the 6-foot-10 Johnson—nicknamed "The Big Unit"—recorded the franchise's first no-hitter on June 2, 1990. That was the start of great things, as Johnson would go on to post a 130–74 record for Seattle over the next 10 years. Along with Buhner, Seattle's "Big Three" of Johnson, Martinez, and Griffey propelled the 1990 Mariners to a respectable 77–85 mark.

FIRST BASEMAN · ALVIN DAVIS

"Mr. Mariner," Alvin Davis, was named the AL Rookie of the Year when he slugged 27 home runs and collected 116 RBI in 1984. The only Mariners player to win a major award in the club's first dozen years, Davis set or tied team records for most RBI, walks, and home runs by a rookie. Hitting most of his homers in the friendly confines of Seattle's Kingdome, the smooth-swinging left-hander was a huge fan favorite in the franchise's early years. His sharp batting eye led to many walks, often raising his on-base percentage more than 100 points above his batting average.

STATS

Mariners seasons: 1984–91

Height: 6-1

Weight: 195

- **.280 career BA**
- **3-time Mariners team MVP**
- **1984 AL Rookie of the Year**
- **1984 All-Star**

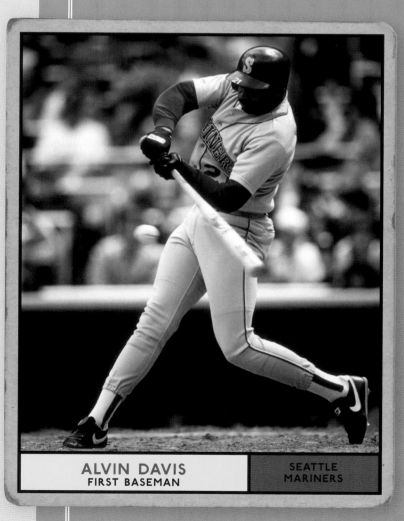

ALVIN DAVIS
FIRST BASEMAN

SEATTLE
MARINERS

RANDY JOHNSON

Randy Johnson reinforced his scary
reputation by leading the league in hit
batsmen in 1992 (18) and 1993 (16).

SECOND BASEMAN · HAROLD REYNOLDS

A defensive stalwart with excellent speed and fielding range, Reynolds led all AL second basemen in games started, fielding chances, putouts, assists, and double plays in 1987. The powerful switch hitter was also terrific at the plate, a keen-eyed batter who rarely struck out and steadily improved his batting average as his career went along. The ever-smiling, community-conscious Reynolds won the 1991 Roberto Clemente Award for his outstanding work with young baseball players. Reynolds retired in 1994, trading in his baseball jersey for a sports jacket to become a television baseball analyst.

HAROLD REYNOLDS
SECOND BASEMAN

SEATTLE
MARINERS

STATS

Mariners seasons: 1983–92

Height: 5-11

Weight: 165

- **2-time All-Star**

- **3-time Gold Glove winner**

- **1987 AL leader in stolen bases (60)**

- **1988 AL leader in triples (11)**

Seattle's fortunes continued to rise in 1991 as the Mariners avoided a losing record for the first time in their history, finishing the season 83–79. "We're not losers anymore!" yelled Alvin Davis as the Kingdome crowd went wild after victory number 81. So enthusiastic was the fans' response that Dave Niehaus, who had been the Mariners radio broadcaster since 1977, noted, "It was like we'd won the World Series."

Expectations rose higher as former big-league outfielder Lou Piniella was then hired as Seattle's manager. The fiery Piniella had skippered the Cincinnati Reds to a 1990 World Series title, and Seattle fans hoped he would bring the same magic to the Mariners. It would not happen right away, though, as a winning 1993 season (82–80) was sandwiched between two losing ones.

During a game in July 1994, four large ceiling tiles crashed down from the Kingdome roof, forcing the Mariners onto the longest road trip in franchise history—20 away games in 21 days. As the team embarked on the grueling schedule, Seattle officials began discussing the possible building of a new baseball stadium. Rumors also began to swirl that the Mariners might relocate to the greener pastures of another city. Seattle needed a special season, and it was about to get one.

KEN GRIFFEY SR.

LIKE FATHER, LIKE SON

On August 31, 1990, the Seattle Mariners made family history. For the first time, a father and son—outfielders Ken Griffey Sr. and Ken Griffey Jr.—played in the same major-league lineup. The 40-year-old and 20-year-old, batting second and third in Seattle's lineup, did not disappoint. In the first inning, the packed Kingdome crowd rose to its feet when Griffey Sr. knocked a hit up the middle for a single, and it jumped up again when Griffey Jr. ripped a single to right field. When Griffey Sr. scored the first run of the game on a hit by first baseman Alvin Davis, and Griffey Jr. scored the second run just a few minutes later, the place went wild. In the sixth inning, the elder Griffey showed his son how it was done in the field, throwing out Kansas City Royals outfielder Bo Jackson, who was trying to stretch a single into a double. Griffey Jr. hunched down on his hands and knees in center field and broke into a beaming smile as Jackson was tagged. "I wanted to cry," Junior said. "It was my dad's day." The father-son duo led the Mariners to a 5–2 win that day and played together in a total of 51 games.

KEN GRIFFEY JR.

THIRD BASEMAN · EDGAR MARTINEZ

When the Seattle Mariners were in danger of being relocated in 1995, Edgar Martinez came to the rescue. His series-clinching double down the left-field line in the ALDS helped propel the Mariners to a new level of popularity in Seattle. A skilled fielder and patient hitter, Martinez—known as "Papi" or "Gar" to his teammates—usually looked over several pitches before deciding which one to attack. The soft-spoken native of Puerto Rico earned renown as one of the AL's top designated hitters but also spent nearly 600 games manning third base.

STATS

Mariners seasons: 1987–2004

Height: 6-0

Weight: 218

- **7-time All-Star**
- **2004 Roberto Clemente Award winner**
- **2-time AL leader in BA**
- **309 career HR**

EDGAR MARTINEZ
THIRD BASEMAN

SEATTLE
MARINERS

CHANGE OF COURSE

hen Griffey was sidelined with a broken wrist, Seattle's 1995 season seemed in trouble. To get a much-needed boost on the mound, the Mariners then traded two minor-league prospects to the San Diego Padres for consistent starter Andy Benes. "We really feel that this is the big year for us with the pennant race and the Wild Card race," said Mariners executive Roger Jongewaard.

By August, the Mariners were 13 games behind the California Angels in the AL West race. But an Angels losing streak then coincided with a Mariners winning rampage. Behind veterans such as Johnson and Martinez, Seattle miraculously charged back, defeating the Angels 9–1 in a special one-game playoff to secure its first division title. The underdog Mariners then kept right on rolling in the playoffs, beating the New York Yankees in an AL Division Series (ALDS) marked by one of the most exciting finishes in postseason history. In the deciding Game 5, Griffey—back from his injury—slammed a home run in the eighth inning to send the game into extra innings, then scored the game-winning run on a Martinez double in the bottom of the 11th.

Baseball hysteria in Seattle reached a fever pitch as the team was victorious in two of the first three AL Championship Series (ALCS) games against the Cleveland Indians. The excitement subsided, though, as the Indians

JAY BUHNER

REFUSE TO LOSE

In mid-August 1995, the Mariners were rumored to be on the verge of being sold and moved to Tampa Bay, Florida, when, suddenly, the team started winning. A 13-game deficit to the California Angels slowly was whittled away until the "September to Remember" had captured the hearts and imaginations of baseball fans throughout the Pacific Northwest. During this miraculous run, Seattle fans and players adopted "Refuse to lose" as their motto. With sold-out crowds packing the Kingdome for every home game, it often seemed that the club never did lose. Seattle fans came to the ballpark wondering which player was going to win it for them that night. Ken Griffey Jr.'s triumphant return in August after a wrist injury sparked one of the greatest team comebacks in major-league history, and he and players such as Jay Buhner, Dan Wilson, and Edgar Martinez took turns playing the hero. The team didn't stop winning until it had captured the first AL West crown in franchise history with a 9–1, one-game playoff victory over the Angels in a jam-packed Kingdome in the season's last game. "We may not have had the best team," said Seattle infielder Rich Amaral, "but we knew we were going to win."

swept the next three games to capture the pennant. The ride was over in Seattle, but what a ride it had been; that 1995 season is still fondly remembered in Seattle as "The Magical Season."

In 1996, the Mariners welcomed an extraordinary rookie shortstop named Alex Rodriguez. "A-Rod," as he was known, was a graceful defender with a powerful arm and an explosive bat. "Alex has a good chance to be the best shortstop ever," said Baltimore Orioles Hall of Fame shortstop Cal Ripken Jr. Seattle's star-studded lineup went on to win a team-record 85 games that season, but a second-place finish in the division left the Mariners out of the playoffs.

DAN WILSON – Throughout a 12-year Mariners career, Wilson was known for his solid defense and steady play. His strong throwing arm kept opposing base runners in check, and his occasional pop at the plate helped Seattle win three AL West titles.

Randy Johnson was among baseball's top stories in 1997, as he notched a 20–4 record and 291 strikeouts. Seattle's mighty offense also clobbered a franchise-record 264 home runs that year, and the team sent five players to the All-Star Game: Johnson, Griffey, Martinez, Rodriguez, and 5-foot-8 second baseman Joey Cora. The Mariners' season ended with another AL West championship and a return to the postseason, but the team quickly fell to the Baltimore Orioles in the first round of the playoffs. The playoff loss hurt, but fans found two more reasons to cheer as Griffey was named AL Most Valuable Player (MVP) after racking up 56 homers and 147 RBI, and construction began on a new stadium that would ensure the Mariners remained in Seattle.

In 1998, Mariners pitcher Jamie Moyer earned his 100th career win and 1,000th strikeout, and Griffey became the youngest player ever to slam his 350th home run. Still, the season ended in disappointment, as the club finished 11 and a half games out of the AL West race.

The main highlight of the 1999 season occurred on July 15, when the Mariners moved into Safeco Field, their new, state-of-the-art stadium in downtown Seattle. The gorgeous park, built at a cost of $518 million, was created to lure more fans and enable Seattle to sign more top-notch players. Many Seattle fans were therefore left puzzled—and heartbroken—when the club parted with two of its greatest heroes. By 1999, fans had bid farewell to both Randy Johnson and Ken Griffey Jr.

SHORTSTOP · ALEX RODRIGUEZ

"A-Rod" was one of baseball's brightest stars almost immediately upon joining the Mariners at 18 years of age, quickly proving himself a superb all-around player who could hit, field, run, and throw equally well. Tall, long-armed, and powerful, Rodriguez could hit almost any pitch for a home run. In 1998, he became just the third member (after baseball greats Jose Canseco and Barry Bonds) of the "40-40" club (40 home runs and 40 stolen bases), racking up 42 dingers and 46 steals. He won four Silver Slugger awards as baseball's top-hitting shortstop during his years with the Mariners.

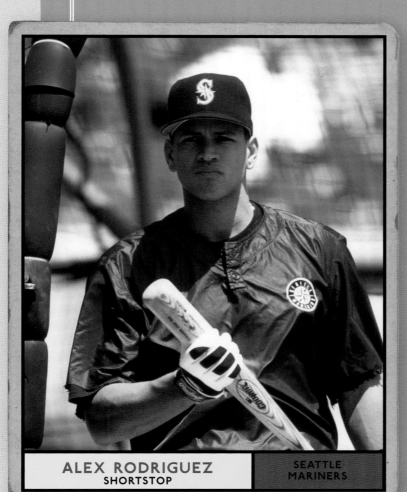

ALEX RODRIGUEZ
SHORTSTOP

SEATTLE
MARINERS

STATS

Mariners seasons: 1994–2000

Height: 6-3

Weight: 225

- **1996 AL leader in BA (.358)**

- **2-time Gold Glove winner**

- **241 career stolen bases**

- **4-time AL leader in HR**

Quick, rangy, and strong-armed, Alex Rodriguez quickly became one of baseball's top defensive infielders.

EDGAR MARTINEZ

THE DOUBLE

One of the most memorable moments in Mariners history happened in the deciding Game 5 of the 1995 ALDS. It was the bottom of the 11th inning, and Seattle trailed the New York Yankees 5–4. Mariners second baseman Joey Cora was on third base, center fielder Ken Griffey Jr. was on first, and powerful designated hitter Edgar Martinez was at the plate. Yankees pitcher Jack McDowell delivered, and Martinez smoked a line drive down the Kingdome's left-field line. Griffey, flying at the crack of the bat, touched second base before the ball even hit the outfield wall. The Seattle crowd stood as one as Cora sped for home with Griffey suddenly hot on his heels. Cora touched home, Griffey slid across the plate in a dusty blur, and the Mariners won the game 6–5, setting off an explosion of cheers. Martinez's clutch two-bagger has been immortalized since then as simply "The Double." That one hit sent the Mariners to their first ALCS and helped renew enthusiasm for a new Mariners stadium. Dave Niehaus, the Mariners' play-by-play radio announcer, summed up the famous moment by saying, "That was the biggest hit in Mariners history. There would not be a Safeco Field without it."

MARINERS

MIKE CAMERON

Mike Cameron set a Seattle record with 176 strikeouts in 2002 but also slammed 4 home runs in one game that year.

AROUND THE HORN

he 21st century arrived as a fresh breeze for the Mariners. Griffey was gone, but new center fielder Mike Cameron wowed fans with his incredible glove work and solid hitting. Other talented newcomers included pitcher Freddy Garcia, first baseman David Bell, and Kazuhiro Sasaki, a closer from Japan who anchored the bullpen with 37 saves in 2000. This crew surprised fans by going 91–71, earning a Wild Card berth into the 2000 playoffs, sweeping the Chicago White Sox in the ALDS, and then pushing the Yankees to six games in the ALCS before finally falling.

Seattle fans were then left disappointed by the departure of yet another superstar when Alex Rodriguez jumped to the Texas Rangers for the richest sports contract ever: $252 million for 10 seasons. "I see little connection between superstars and winning," Mariners official Howard Lincoln said, explaining the club's philosophy of balanced team play. "It turns players on to have a team where everyone is expected to contribute."

Two talented players, slugging second baseman Bret Boone and speedy Japanese outfielder Ichiro Suzuki, joined the Mariners' roster in 2001. Boone finished the season with a league-leading 141 RBI, an AL record for second baseman. Ichiro, meanwhile, put on a stunning all-around performance. The

LEFT FIELDER · JAY BUHNER

Jay Buhner had his flaws. He led the AL in strikeouts in 1996 and 1997, and he was so slow that he managed just six stolen bases in his career. But the outfielder made up for it with his home run power, clubhouse leadership, and cannon of a throwing arm. Seattle fans adored Buhner—recognizable by his shaved head and wraparound sunglasses—for his friendly personality and great passion for the game. He manned primarily right field but spent time in left as well and played defense with such intensity that even his slow feet could not keep him from winning a Gold Glove award in 1996.

JAY BUHNER
LEFT FIELDER

SEATTLE
MARINERS

STATS

Mariners seasons: 1988–2001

Height: 6-3

Weight: 205

- **965 career RBI**

- **3 seasons of 40-plus HR**

- **1996 All-Star**

- **.383 BA in 1995 playoffs**

BASEBALL HEAVEN

Before the 2001 season, no one could have guessed that the Seattle Mariners were about to become the first team since the 1906 Chicago Cubs to win 116 regular-season games and, in the process, captivate an entire city. Local enthusiasm became so great during the season that one Spokane Valley farmer even transformed a 14-acre corn field into a maze shaped like the Mariners' compass logo. That "season in baseball heaven," as it is remembered in Mariners country, featured many stars. Ichiro Suzuki sustained an amazing 23-game hitting streak, Freddy Garcia notched 163 strikeouts, and Mike Cameron hit 25 home runs. By early June, with Seattle leading the AL West by 19 games, the question was not whether Seattle would win the division, but by how many games. Seattle fans were shocked when the Mariners fell behind the Cleveland Indians two games to one in the opening round of the playoffs. But manager Lou Piniella's crew came back to beat the Tribe in five games and reach the ALCS for a rematch with the New York Yankees. The Yankees showed no respect for the record-setting Mariners, though, beating them in five games and putting an end to the dream season.

lithe, quiet right fielder with the laser throwing arm made a spectacular debut with a 23-game hitting streak in his first big-league season. Ichiro went on to win the AL Rookie of the Year award as well as the Gold Glove award for his excellent defense, becoming the first major-leaguer in 26 years to win such honors in the same season.

With the contributions of these new players, the 2001 Mariners dominated the AL West and set a new AL record for wins in a season with 116, losing only 46 games all year. In the ALDS, the Mariners overcame a slow start to beat the Indians and advance to the ALCS against the Yankees. Frustratingly, for the second year in a row, New York stopped the Mariners, ending their storybook season by winning four of five games. Seattle fans didn't know it yet, but that was the last playoff action the Mariners would see for a while.

Longtime manager Lou Piniella jumped ship in 2002 to become skipper of his hometown Tampa Bay Devil Rays, and the Mariners hired Bob Melvin as his replacement. In 2003, Seattle led the division in the second half of the season but then saw the title slip away. For the second year in a row, the Mariners went an impressive 93–69 but missed the playoffs. Still, fans remained justly proud of their team and its fourth straight winning campaign. As one Mariners fan put it at season's end, "Showing up this weekend at Safeco is our way of saying, 'Hey, thanks for all the good times.'"

Although the Mariners fell to a disappointing 63–99 in 2004, there was

CENTER FIELDER · KEN GRIFFEY JR.

Ken Griffey Jr., nicknamed "The Kid," was the darling of Mariners fans in the 1990s when the team emerged as a playoff contender and was voted "Player of the Decade" by his major-league peers. Griffey often made breathtaking, over-the-shoulder catches of the sort immortalized by New York Giants center fielder Willie Mays during the 1954 World Series.

At the plate, he displayed one of the most effortlessly powerful swings of all time. "Junior" made history by playing on the same Mariners team as his talented outfielder father, Ken Griffey Sr., in 1990 and 1991. Father and son even hit back-to-back home runs on September 14, 1990.

STATS

Mariners seasons: 1989–99

Height: 6-3

Weight: 218

- **12-time All-Star**
- **10-time Gold Glove winner**
- **1,608 career RBI**
- **563 career HR**

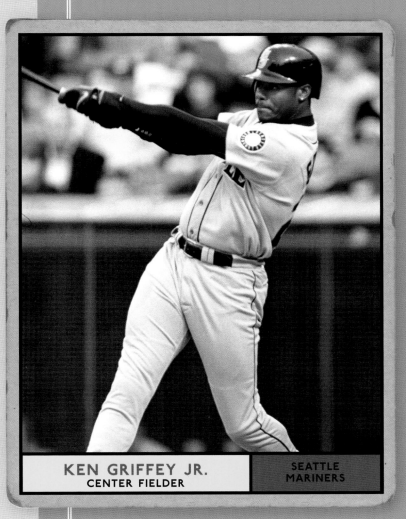

KEN GRIFFEY JR.
CENTER FIELDER

SEATTLE
MARINERS

RIGHT FIELDER · ICHIRO SUZUKI

After playing nine years with the Orix Blue Wave in Japan's Pacific League, Ichiro Suzuki became the first Japanese position player to sign with a major-league club. He topped the All-Star balloting in his rookie season (largely because fan voting was allowed in Japan) and earned the 2001 Rookie of the Year award. In the field, the slender Ichiro fired throws with laser precision, and he featured a most unique style at the plate. The momentum from his left-handed swing propelled him toward first base even as he was making contact, forcing infielders to rush their throws to try to gun him down.

STATS

Mariners seasons: 2001–present

Height: 5-9

Weight: 172

- **6-time All-Star**
- **6-time Gold Glove winner**
- **.331 career BA**
- **235 career stolen bases**

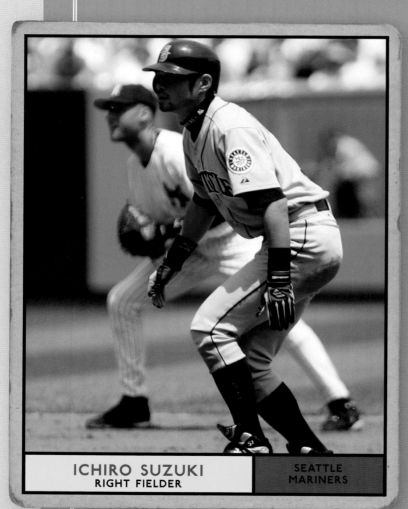

ICHIRO SUZUKI
RIGHT FIELDER

SEATTLE
MARINERS

at least one reason to celebrate. In October, Ichiro Suzuki broke St. Louis Browns great George Sisler's single-season record of 257 hits, finishing with 262. "I'm not a big guy, or muscular, and hopefully kids will look at me and see that somebody with a regular body can get into the record books," the Japanese-speaking Ichiro said through a translator.

The Mariners entered the 2005 season with Mike Hargrove as manager and a rebuilt lineup that featured such quality players as longtime pitcher Jamie Moyer, third baseman Adrian Beltre, and 6-foot-8 first baseman Richie Sexson. Hargrove, who had led the Indians past the Mariners in the 1995 ALCS, believed in the team's chances for speedy improvement. "I'm encouraged by

JAMIE MOYER

JAMIE MOYER – Moyer struggled for a decade in the big leagues before finding his groove in Seattle. In his 11 seasons (1996–2006) in the Emerald City, he won a total of 148 games, using slow-moving but well-placed pitches to keep hitters guessing.

SPECTACULAR SAFECO

Since its inaugural Mariners game on July 15, 1999, Safeco Field has gained a reputation locally and nationally as a terrific, fan-friendly setting for baseball. Breathtaking sunsets and sweeping panoramas of the Seattle skyline, combined with excellent views of the outfield action from all angles, make Safeco Field a stadium unequalled in its visual offerings. The ballpark's one-of-a-kind retractable roof opens and closes like a well-vented convertible, covering the stands and the field but preserving an open-air environment. The structure of Safeco Field covers nearly nine acres and contains enough steel to build a skyscraper 55 stories tall, while the playing field features real Kentucky bluegrass and a specially designed watering system that resembles a spider web. Other unique features include cedar-lined dugouts, elevated bullpens, 11 video display boards, an old-fashioned, hand-operated scoreboard, and many high-tech kiosks and luxury suites equipped with Internet access. The stadium features a wide walking and viewing concourse area that allows fans to make a complete circle of the ballpark while snacking on salmon sandwiches, clam chowder, and sushi rolls. Works of art such as a sculpture of 1,000 bats suspended above the grand staircase at the Home Plate Gate also decorate the unique ballpark.

MANAGER · LOU PINIELLA

Lou Piniella, nicknamed "Sweet Lou," was a fiery left fielder with a pretty swing. Piniella manned the outfield for the expansion Seattle Pilots and then played for the Orioles, Indians, Royals, and Yankees in the 1970s before launching a successful managerial career. Piniella went on to become the winningest manager in Mariners history, gaining his 234th victory on May 22, 1996, against the Boston Red Sox. Piniella was a brilliant game strategist; however, his explosive temper made him one of the most frequently ejected managers in big-league history. Piniella once threw second base into the outfield in an argument with an umpire.

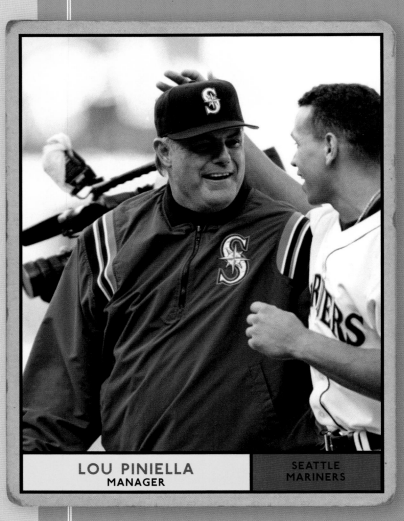

LOU PINIELLA
MANAGER

SEATTLE
MARINERS

STATS

Mariners seasons as manager: 1993–2002

Height: 6-2

Weight: 198

Managerial Record: 1,519–1,420

AL West Championships: 1995, 1997, 2001

Although a solid fielder, Richie Sexson really earned his pay at the plate, hitting 39 homers with 121 RBI in 2005.

RICHIE SEXSON

FELIX HERNANDEZ

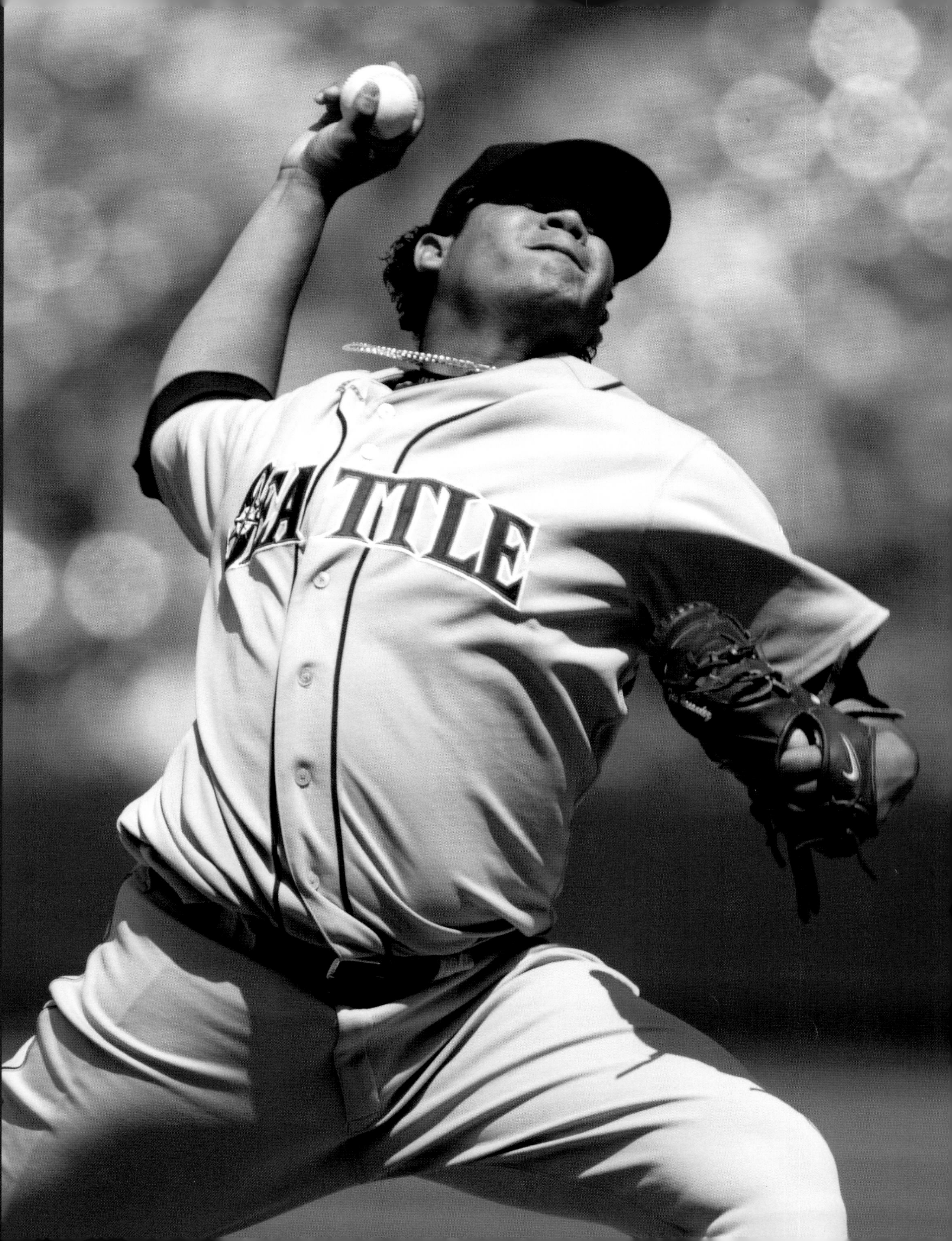

what we've got," he said, "but we have to be consistent from day one."

Consistency would be lacking in 2005, but the season featured at least one exciting moment. On August 3, teenage pitcher Felix Hernandez was called up from the minor leagues. Hernandez's blistering fastball, sharp-breaking curveball, and tantalizing changeup gave Mariners fans an indication of why the 19-year-old was the highest-rated pitching prospect in all of baseball.

The Mariners showed improvement in 2005 and 2006, going 69–93 and then 78–84. The team's increase in wins, along with the 2006 emergence of such rising stars as versatile second baseman Jose Lopez and slick-fielding shortstop Yuniesky Betancourt, made Hargrove as optimistic as Seattle's fans. "I believe we have a chance to do some really good things this year," the manager said before the start of spring training in 2007. "I'm really, honestly, excited to get to work."

The Seattle Mariners have produced some of baseball's greatest players and moments, but the team has yet to achieve the ultimate pinnacle of winning, or even reaching, a World Series. Today's baseball heroes with the compass logo on their chests hope to play beautiful baseball in the scenic Pacific Northwest and finally reel in the big fish that's been eluding them.

INDEX